Food Science Consultant

Shirley Corriher

For Abigail, CF
For my own Wizard Dad, HR

My Dad's a WIZARD!

Written by
Hannah Roche

Illustrated by
Chris Fisher

My dad's a wizard!

Today he did a very weird thing.
He put lots of empty bowls in
the freezer!

Then he took some strawberries
and pushed them through a strainer
to make them mushy. I stirred in
some sugar and lemon juice.

Next Dad whipped some cream until it made little mountains in the bowl.

And bit by bit, very gently, he stirred some cream into my fruit. We poured it all into one of the cold bowls and put it in the freezer.

Then we started all over again –

first with peaches,
next with raspberries,
then with bananas...

my favorite!

We had to wait for a long time.
First the stuff was all mushy, then
just slushy with little bits of ice.

We had to stir the bowls two times.
Finally, Dad said they were just right –
frozen, but soft enough to spoon out.

Then Dad got the biggest cold bowl.
He put the strawberry in the bottom,
then the peach,
then the raspberry.
I put the banana on top.

There was a lot of waiting in-between,
for everything to freeze – Dad's cooking
always has a lot of waiting in it.

Finally, Dad said it was time.
He took the bowl out of the freezer.
"Watch this magic!" he said, and
dipped the bowl in some hot water.

Then **Abracadabra!**

He turned it upside down
and out came the **ice cream**,
like a big sandcastle with stripes!

We put some fruit on top...and a flag.

I love my wizard dad!

Notes for Parents

EVEN very young children are aware that water is wet, rock is hard, sand is grainy. As they observe more, children discover that things don't always stay the same – whipping, heating, mixing, freezing and so on make things change from watery to fluffy, from soft to hard, from liquid to solid....

LEARNING to notice and describe the textures and changes is important to children's understanding of the world around them. Don't worry about using "proper" scientific words – getting the description right is what really matters.

YOU can recreate the story in your own kitchen by following the recipe opposite. As you go along, encourage your child to talk about what's happening. Then, you can eat the results!

HOW IT WORKS

WHEN a liquid starts to freeze, the particles in it vibrate less energetically as the temperature drops. First they form little clumps, then they fuse together into a tightly knit, solid structure.

PLUNGING the bowl of ice cream into hot water melts the ice cream immediately inside the edge of the bowl. Because the center remains solid, it slides out as one piece.

Jessie's Recipe

YOU WILL NEED:

2 cups of strawberries, leaves removed, *or*

3 peaches, peeled and finely chopped, *or*

2 cups of raspberries, *or*

2 ripe bananas, mashed

1 teaspoon of lemon juice

1 cup of confectioners sugar

⅔ cup of heavy cream

a large strainer, a whisk or electric mixer,

1 large bowl, 4 small bowls, some large

spoons and extra bowls

HINTS

PUTTING the bowls in the freezer before you begin gives better results.

STIR the mixture well at least twice during freezing to prevent ice particles from forming and to prevent the fruit sinking.

1. Put the large bowl and the 4 small bowls in the freezer.

2. Push the fruit through the strainer, then add the sugar and lemon juice.

3. Whip the cream (with the whisk or the electric mixer) until it forms soft peaks, then gently fold it into the fruit mixture.

4. Pour the mixture into a small bowl from the freezer and return to the freezer.

5. After 90 minutes, take it out, gently stir the mixture, and return it to the freezer. After an hour, stir the ice cream again and continue to freeze for another hour.

6. To make the layered ice cream you will need to do steps 2–5 with each fruit.

7. Then take all the bowls out of the freezer and layer the ice creams in the big bowl. Freeze this for at least another hour.

8. When the ice cream is firm, dip the bowl in hot water for a few seconds, and turn it upside down over a large plate.